----------------------------------------

From

----------------------------------------

Written and compiled by Sophie Piper
Illustrations copyright © 2012
Kay Widdowson
This edition copyright © 2012
Lion Hudson

The moral rights of the author and
illustrator have been asserted

A Lion Children's Book
an imprint of
**Lion Hudson plc**
Wilkinson House, Jordan Hill Road,
Oxford OX2 8DR, England
www.lionhudson.com
ISBN 978 0 7459 6288 7

First edition 2012
10 9 8 7 6 5 4 3 2 1 0

**Acknowledgments**
Every effort has been made to trace and
contact copyright owners for material
used in this book. We apologize for any
inadvertent omissions or errors.

All unattributed prayers are by Sophie
Piper, copyright © Lion Hudson.

Prayers by Lois Rock are copyright ©
Lion Hudson.
Bible extracts are taken or adapted
from the Good News Bible published by
the Bible Societies and HarperCollins
Publishers, © American Bible Society 1994,
used with permission.

A catalogue record for this book is available
from the British Library

Typeset in 15/20 Baskerville Regular
Printed in China January 2012
(manufacturer LH17)

Distributed by:
UK: Marston Book Services Ltd,
PO Box 269, Abingdon, Oxon OX14 4YN
USA: Trafalgar Square Publishing,
814 N Franklin Street, Chicago, IL 60610
USA Christian Market: Kregel
Publications, PO Box 2607, Grand Rapids,
MI 49501

# First Prayers
# at Bedtime

Sophie Piper

*Illustrated by* Kay Widdowson

LION
CHILDREN'S

# Contents

Day is done,
Gone the sun
From the lake,
From the hills,
From the sky.
Safely rest,
All is well!
God is nigh.

With God you must let things begin,
With God let all things come to rest;
In this way the work of your hands
Will flourish and also be blessed.

Day has ended
dark descended
daytime's troubles
all are mended.

So tomorrow
I may start
glad in mind
and soul and heart.

14

I see the moon
And the moon sees me;
God bless the moon
And God bless me.

The moon shines clear as silver,
The sun shines bright like gold,
And both are very lovely,
And very, very old.

God hung them up as lanterns,
For all beneath the sky;
And nobody can blow them out,
For they are up too high.

Now the day is over,
Night is drawing nigh.
Shadows of the evening
Steal across the sky.

Now the darkness gathers,
Stars begin to peep,
Birds and beasts and flowers
Soon will be asleep.

Through the long night-watches
May the angels spread
Their white wings above me,
Watching round my bed.

20

Dear Father, hear and bless
your beasts and singing birds;
and guard with tenderness
small things that have no words.

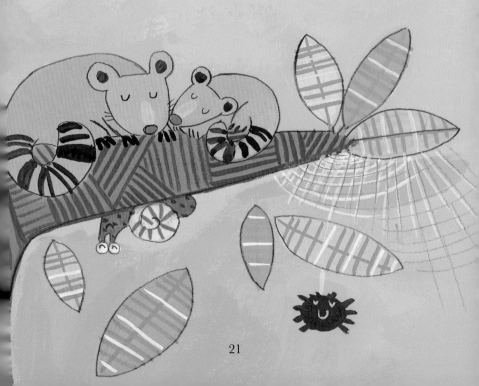

Shadows in the hallway
Shadows on the stair
God be always with me
God be everywhere.

24

An evening prayer
as the sun sinks low:
we thank you, God,
for this world below.

An evening prayer
as the dark comes nigh:
we thank you, God,
for your heaven on high.

Dear God, hear my evening prayer:
Bless me with your love and care.

Let me dream the night away
Until it is another day.

Though tomorrow may be long,
Keep me safe from doing wrong.

May I spend the hours of light
Doing what is good and right.

Jesus, friend of little children,
Be a friend to me;
Take my hand, and ever keep me
Close to thee.

Dear God, you are my shepherd,
You give me all I need,
You take me where the grass grows green
And I can safely feed.

You take me where the water
Is quiet and cool and clear;
And there I rest and know I'm safe
For you are always near.

I love you
and you love me
you and me
together we

like to wander
hand in hand
like to stop
and simply stand

like to chatter
like to play
like to dream
the hours away

like to watch
the fading light
hug and kiss
and say
goodnight.

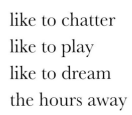

God bless all those that I love;
God bless all those that love me;
God bless all those that love those that I love,
And all those that love those that love me.

God bless Gran
through the bright blue day.
God bless Gran
through the dark grey night.
God bless Gran
when we hug together.
God bless Gran
when we're out of sight.

Keep watch, dear Lord,
with those who work,
or wait, or weep this night;

and may the dark
hold no more fear
than if it were the light.

40

God bless the house from roof to ground,
With love encircle it around.
God bless each window, bless each door,
Be Thou our home for evermore.

Lord, keep us safe this night,
Secure from all our fears;
May angels guard us while we sleep,
Till morning light appears.

Now I lay me down to sleep,
I pray thee, Lord, thy child to keep;
Thy love to guard me through the night
And wake me in the morning light.

The moon shines bright,
The stars give light
Before the break of day;
God bless you all
Both great and small
And send a joyful day.